International Cooking Collection

Favorite Cakes

International Cooking Collection

Favorite Cakes

Jane Suthering

CONTENTS

Published exclusively for Cupress (Canada) Ltd
20 Torbay Road, Markham, Ontario L3R 1G6 Canada
by Woodhead-Faulkner (Publishers) Ltd, Simon & Schuster International Group

This edition first published 1988

ISBN 0-920691-84-6
Printed and bound in Italy

INTRODUCTION

Trends in cake-making and eating have changed over recent years as people have become more conscious of their diet. There is no way round the fact that cakes do contain calories! But, if chosen well, the basic ingredients can all be nutritious, and there are ways a cake can be made more healthy but still look and taste good.

Instead of always frosting cakes, try other ways of decorating: top the mixture with fresh fruit before baking; sprinkle with nuts; simply dust with powdered sugar—1 tablespoon goes a long way; arrange the mixture in the pans in some sort of pattern, either by coloring a portion or by using two completely different mixtures and layering or marbling them together.

A cake is only as good as its ingredients, so choose them well. Perfect results are achieved only by precise attention to detail, so measure the ingredients accurately, use the correct size pan and cook at the specified temperature. Above all, read the recipe through carefully before starting to bake.

I've enjoyed creating this collection of recipes with a more healthy approach. I hope you enjoy them too.

NOTES

All spoon measurements are level.

Ovens should be preheated to the temperature specified.

Quantities of pastry refer to total weight; use either fresh, or frozen pastry that has been thawed.

Basic recipes are marked with an asterisk and given in the reference section (pages 77–9). Increase or decrease the basic quantities in proportion to obtain the amount required.

Use U.S. grade large eggs unless otherwise stated.

If fresh yeast is unobtainable, substitute dried yeast but halve the quantity and use according to the manufacturer's directions.

Unless otherwise stated, level the surface of the cake mixture in the pan with the back of a metal spoon.

Leave the cake in the pan to cool slightly before turning out onto a rack to cool completely.

Remove the lining paper when the cake is cold.

Invert the pan over the cake as it cools on the rack to help keep it moist.

CARDAMOM CAKE

1½ cups all-purpose flour
2 teaspoons baking powder
2 teaspoons ground cardamom
½ cup butter
¾ cup superfine sugar
1 egg, beaten
½ cup sour cream

Serves 8–10
Preparation time: 30 minutes
Cooking time: 55–60 minutes
Freezing: Recommended

1. Grease a 7 inch round loose-bottomed cake pan and line the base.
2. Sift the flour, baking powder and cardamom together. Rub in the butter until the mixture resembles fine crumbs, then stir in the sugar. Weigh ¼ lb of the mixture and set aside.
3. Add the egg and sour cream to the remaining mixture and beat well. Transfer to the prepared pan and sprinkle with the reserved dry mixture.
4. Bake in a 350°F oven for 55–60 minutes. Cool on a rack.

ALMOND AND CHERRY CAKE

An extremely moist cake which keeps well.

¾ cup butter
¾ cup superfine sugar
3 eggs, beaten
1 cup ground almonds
⅔ cup ground rice
½ cup self-rising flour
1 cup halved glacé cherries

Serves 14–16
Preparation time: 35 minutes
Cooking time: About 1¾ hours
Freezing: Recommended

1. Grease a 7 inch round cake pan and line the base.
2. Cream the butter and sugar together until pale and fluffy. Beat in the eggs a little at a time.
3. Sift the dry ingredients together. Toss the cherries in about a quarter of the mixture.
4. Fold the remaining sifted ingredients into the creamed mixture, then carefully fold in the tossed cherries.
5. Transfer to the prepared pan and bake in a 325°F oven for about 1¾ hours, until a skewer inserted into the center of the cake comes out clean. Cool on a rack.

CREAM-FILLED SPONGE CAKE

3 eggs
1 teaspoon grated lemon rind (optional)
1 tablespoon hot water
1/3 cup superfine sugar
2/3 cup all-purpose flour
1 tablespoon cornstarch
2 tablespoons butter, melted
FOR THE FILLING:
6 tablespoons raspberry jam
2/3 cup heavy cream, whipped
powdered sugar to dust

Serves 8
Preparation time: 30 minutes
Cooking time: 20–25 minutes
Freezing: Recommended

1. Grease an 8 inch round cake pan and line the base. Sprinkle the side with superfine sugar, then shake out excess.
2. Place the eggs, lemon rind, if using, hot water and sugar in a large bowl over a pan of simmering water. Using a hand-held electric beater, beat for 5–10 minutes until very thick and pale and the beater leaves a trail through the mixture. Remove from the heat.
3. Sift the flour and cornstarch together, then fold into the mixture. Fold in the melted butter.
4. Transfer the mixture to the prepared pan. Bake in a 375°F oven for 20–25 minutes, until risen and just firm to the touch. Cool on a rack.
5. Split the cake horizontally and sandwich together with the jam and cream. Dust with powdered sugar.

CHOCOLATE VARIATION

Omit lemon rind. Replace 2 tablespoons flour with cocoa powder. Add 1 teaspoon instant coffee to the hot water.

BRAZIL NUT AND COFFEE CAKE

3/4 cup butter
3/4 cup light brown sugar, packed
3 eggs
2 cups all-purpose flour
1 tablespoon baking powder
1 cup slivered brazil nuts, toasted
1 tablespoon instant coffee, dissolved in 2 tablespoons boiling water
FOR THE FILLING AND TOPPING:
2 teaspoons powdered sugar
2 teaspoons instant coffee, dissolved in 2 teaspoons boiling water
1 cup heavy cream, lightly whipped
12 sugared coffee beans or other coffee candy

1. Grease two 8 inch round cake pans and line the bases.
2. Cream the butter and sugar together until pale and fluffy. Beat in the eggs one at a time.
3. Sift the flour and baking powder together, then add the brazils. Fold into the creamed mixture, then fold in the coffee.
4. Divide the mixture between the prepared pans and bake in a 350°F oven for about 25 minutes, until risen and firm to the touch. Cool on a rack.
5. Meanwhile, make the filling. Stir the sugar into the coffee, then stir into the cream. Cut one of the cakes into 12 sections. Using one third of the cream, pipe a swirl on each section. Top each swirl with a sugared coffee bean or candy.
6. Place the whole cake on a serving plate and cover with the remaining cream. Arrange the sections on top.

Serves 12
Preparation time:
45 minutes
Cooking time:
About 25 minutes
Freezing:
Recommended, without sugared coffee beans

COCONUT SLICE

This cake has a low proportion of flour, so the combination of coconut, eggs and butter makes it very moist and crumbly.

½ cup butter
½ cup superfine sugar
2 tablespoons warm water
2 eggs, beaten
¾ cup self-rising flour
½ teaspoon baking powder
1 cup flaked coconut, plus 2 tablespoons for sprinkling

Serves 10
Preparation time: 25 minutes
Cooking time: About 35 minutes
Freezing: Recommended

1. Grease a 6½ × 3¾ × 3 inch loaf pan and line the base.
2. Cream the butter and sugar together until pale and fluffy. Beat in the water 1 tablespoon at a time. Beat in the eggs a little at a time.
3. Sift the flour and baking powder together, then add the flaked coconut. Fold into the creamed mixture, then transfer to the prepared pan.
4. Make a slight dip in the center then sprinkle the surface with the remaining coconut.
5. Bake in a 350°F oven for about 35 minutes, until risen and firm to the touch. Cool on a rack.
6. Cut into thick slices to serve.

DATE, WALNUT AND BANANA LOAF

The combination of date, walnut and banana is a childhood memory which is just as pleasing today. The full flavor of this cake develops after a day or so.

½ cup butter
⅔ cup light brown sugar, packed
2 eggs, beaten
3 large, very ripe bananas
2 cups all-purpose flour
1 tablespoon baking powder
¼ teaspoon salt
½ teaspoon ground mace or ground nutmeg
⅔ cup chopped dates
½ cup chopped walnuts

1. Grease a 6½ × 3¾ × 3 inch loaf pan and line the base.
2. Cream the butter and sugar together until pale and fluffy. Beat in the eggs a little at a time.
3. Mash the bananas, then beat into the creamed mixture.
4. Sift the dry ingredients together, then add the dates and walnuts. Fold into the banana mixture.
5. Transfer to a prepared pan and make a slight dip in the center. Bake in a 350°F oven for 50–60 minutes, until risen and firm to the touch. Cool on a rack.
6. Cut into thick slices to serve, buttered if you wish.

Serves 12
Preparation time:
About 30 minutes
Cooking time:
50–60 minutes
Freezing:
Recommended

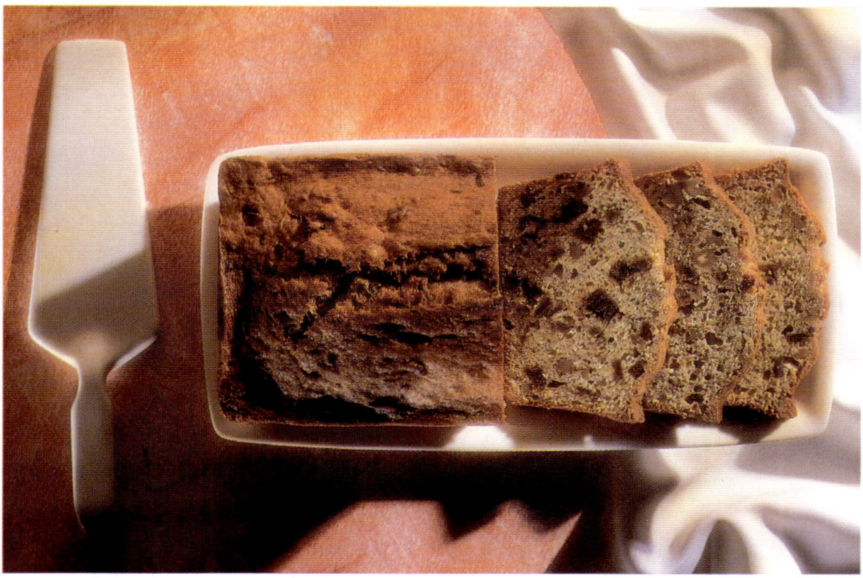

JAMAICAN SURPRISE CAKE

A rich dark spiced cake with a surprising moist coconut center. Include rum for a real Jamaican flavor.

2 egg whites
1/3 cup superfine sugar
1 cup flaked coconut
1/2 cup molasses
3 tablespoons light brown granulated sugar
1/3 cup butter
1 1/2 cups all-purpose flour
1/2 teaspoon baking soda
2 teaspoons ground ginger
1 teaspoon ground mixed spice
2 eggs, beaten
2 tablespoons dark rum, orange juice or milk

Serves 10
Preparation time: 30 minutes
Cooking time: 45–50 minutes
Freezing: Recommended

1. Grease a 7 inch round cake pan and line the base.
2. Place the egg whites, superfine sugar and coconut in a saucepan. Heat gently for a few minutes, stirring carefully with a wooden spoon, until the mixture is hot and the sugar is dissolved—about 140°F on a candy thermometer. Leave until cold.
3. Place the molasses, light brown sugar and butter in a saucepan and heat gently until melted.
4. Sift the dry ingredients together, then add to the butter mixture with the eggs and rum, orange juice or milk. Beat well.
5. Pour half of the mixture into the prepared pan. Spoon the coconut mixture into the center, then pour over the remaining ginger mixture.
6. Bake in a 325°F oven for 45–50 minutes, until risen and firm to the touch. Cool on a rack.

HONEY CAKE

This is a light-textured moist cake with a spiced honey flavor. It improves if kept for a few days before slicing.

2 cups all-purpose flour
1 teaspoon ground cinnamon
1 teaspoon ground mixed spice
1 egg
3/4 cup superfine sugar
1 teaspoon baking soda
1/2 cup freshly squeezed orange juice
1/2 cup honey
1/2 cup vegetable oil

1. Grease a 9 inch square cake pan and line the base.
2. Sift the flour and spices together into a bowl.

3. Place the egg and sugar in a blender or food processor and work until pale and creamy. Transfer to a large mixing bowl, add the sifted ingredients and mix well.
4. Dissolve the baking soda in the orange juice, then stir into the cake mixture. Add the honey and oil and work until smooth.
5. Transfer the mixture to the prepared pan and bake in a 325°F oven for about 45 minutes, until risen and firm to the touch. Cool on a rack.

Serves 16–20
Preparation time:
25 minutes
Cooking time:
About 45 minutes
Freezing:
Recommended

GROUND RICE CAKE

An increasing number of people are allergic to wheat. This recipe contains no wheat flour at all. Choose a special baking powder if necessary.

½ cup butter
½ cup superfine sugar
2 eggs, beaten
1 teaspoon vanilla
3–4 tablespoons milk
1⅓ cups ground rice
1 teaspoon baking powder
powdered sugar for dusting

Serves 10
Preparation: 20 minutes
Cooking time: About 30 minutes
Freezing: Recommended

1. Grease an 8 inch round cake pan and line the base.
2. Cream the butter and sugar together until pale and fluffy. Beat in the eggs a little at a time, then beat in the vanilla. Gradually beat in 3 tablespoons milk.
3. Mix the ground rice and baking powder together and fold into the creamed mixture to give a soft dropping consistency. Add a little extra milk if necessary.
4. Transfer the mixture to the prepared pan and bake in a 350°F oven for about 30 minutes, until risen and firm to the touch. Cool on a rack. Dust with powdered sugar and serve with fresh fruit.

TOFFEE-TOPPED CAKE

¾ cup butter
¾ cup light brown sugar, packed
3 eggs, beaten
1 teaspoon vanilla
1 cup all-purpose flour
1¼ cups self-rising flour
pinch of salt
2 tablespoons milk

FOR THE TOPPING:
3 tablespoons butter
1 tablespoon all-purpose flour
3 tablespoons light brown sugar
⅓ cup finely chopped filberts

Serves 12–16
Preparation time: 30 minutes
Cooking time: About 1¼ hours
Freezing: Recommended

1. Grease and line a 7 inch round cake pan.
2. Cream the butter and sugar until pale and fluffy. Beat in the eggs a little at a time, then beat in the vanilla.
3. Sift the flours and salt together, then fold into the creamed mixture. Fold in the milk to give a dropping consistency. Transfer to the prepared pan.
4. Combine all the topping ingredients and beat well. Sprinkle evenly over the top of the cake.
5. Bake in a 325°F oven for about 1¼ hours, until a skewer inserted into the center of the cake comes out clean. Cool on a rack.

DUNDEE CAKE

This traditional Scottish fruit cake keeps well in a cool, dry place if wrapped in foil and sealed in a plastic bag.

3/4 cup butter
2/3 cup superfine sugar
2 tablespoons orange marmalade
4 eggs, beaten
2 cups all-purpose flour
1 teaspoon baking powder
1/2 cup ground almonds
2 cups golden raisins
1/3 cup cut mixed peel
1/3 cup whole blanched almonds
2 tablespoons whisky

Serves 16
Preparation time: 35 minutes
Cooking time: About 2 hours
Freezing: Suitable, though unnecessary

1. Grease and line a 7 inch round cake pan.
2. Cream the butter and sugar together until pale and fluffy. Beat in the marmalade, then beat in the eggs a little at a time.
3. Sift together the flour, baking powder and ground almonds, then fold into the creamed mixture with the golden raisins and peel. Transfer to the prepared pan, level the surface, then make a slight dip in the center.
4. Arrange the almonds in concentric circles on top.
5. Bake in a 275°F oven for about 2 hours, until a skewer inserted into the center of the cake comes out clean.
6. Pour the whisky over the surface of the cake and leave in the pan for 5 minutes. Cool on a rack.

CHOCOLATE FUDGE CAKE

Instead of sandwiching this cake together with the frosting, use whipped heavy cream and reduce all the frosting ingredients by a third for the covering.

1 1/2 cups all-purpose flour
2 tablespoons cocoa powder
1 teaspoon baking powder
1/2 teaspoon baking soda
2/3 cup light brown sugar, packed
2 tablespoons golden syrup or 1 tablespoon each light corn syrup and molasses
2/3 cup sunflower oil
2/3 cup plain yogurt
2 eggs, beaten
2 oz baker's semi-sweet chocolate, grated
FOR THE FROSTING:
6 oz baker's semi-sweet chocolate, melted
3/4 cup sweet butter
1 1/2 cups sifted powdered sugar

1. Grease two 8½ inch round cake pans and line the bases.
2. Sift the flour, cocoa, baking powder, baking soda and sugar together. Add the remaining ingredients and beat well for about 2 minutes.
3. Divide the mixture between the prepared pans and bake in a 325°F oven for 30 minutes, or until risen and firm to the touch. Cool on a rack.
4. Place the frosting ingredients in a bowl and beat until smooth. Use to fill and cover the cake.

Serves 10
Preparation time:
40 minutes
Cooking time:
About 30 minutes
Freezing:
Recommended; freeze uncovered until solid

SPICED PRUNE CAKE

1/2 cup pitted prunes, soaked overnight in boiling water
1/3 cup butter
3/4 cup light brown sugar, packed
2 eggs, beaten
1 3/4 cups whole wheat flour
2 teaspoons baking powder
1/4 teaspoon baking soda
1/4 teaspoon salt
1 teaspoon ground cinnamon
1/2 teaspoon ground cloves
FOR THE TOPPING:
1/2 cup chopped pitted prunes
2/3 cup water
1/2 cup cream cheese or ricotta cheese
TO DECORATE:
16 orange segments

Serves 16
Preparation time: 50 minutes, plus soaking time
Cooking time: About 40 minutes
Freezing: Recommended, without orange segments; freeze uncovered until solid

1. Grease a 9 inch square cake pan and line the base.
2. Drain the prunes, reserving the liquid. Puree the prunes in a blender or food processor, then transfer to a measuring pitcher. Make up to 1 1/4 cups with the reserved liquid.
3. Cream the butter with half of the sugar until pale and fluffy. Beat in the remaining sugar, then the eggs a little at a time.
4. Stir the dry ingredients together until evenly mixed, then fold into the creamed mixture alternately with the prune puree.
5. Transfer the mixture to the prepared pan and bake in a 350°F oven for about 40 minutes, until risen and firm to the touch. Cool on a rack.
6. Meanwhile, prepare the topping. Place the prunes and water in a small pan and cook gently for about 10 minutes, stirring occasionally, until the water is absorbed and the fruit softened. Beat in the cheese and chill until required.
7. Spread the cake with the topping and cut into 16 squares. Top each with an orange segment to serve.

VARIATION

Replace the prunes with dried apricots for both the cake mixture and the topping.

PLUM AND LEMON SLICES

The plums go beautifully with the rich, lemon-flavored mixture and they create an attractive crackled design on top of the cake. Best sliced and served while still slightly warm.

3 eggs
3/4 cup superfine sugar
grated rind of 1 lemon
pinch of salt
1 3/4 cups self-rising flour
2 tablespoons cornstarch
3/4 cup butter, melted
1 lb plums, quartered and pitted

Serves 12
Preparation time: About 40 minutes
Cooking time: 1–1 1/4 hours
Freezing: Recommended

1. Grease a 10 inch springform cake pan and line the base.
2. Place the eggs, sugar, lemon rind and salt in a large bowl over a pan of simmering water and beat, using a hand-held electric beater, for 5–10 minutes, until very thick and pale and the beater leaves a trail through the mixture. Remove from the heat.
3. Sift the flour and cornstarch together, then fold into the beaten mixture.
4. Fold in all but 1–2 tablespoons of the melted butter. Transfer the mixture to the prepared pan.
5. Arrange the plums decoratively, skin side up, on top of the mixture, then drizzle over the remaining butter.
6. Bake in a 325°F oven for 1–1 1/4 hours, until risen and firm to the touch. Cool on a rack.
7. Serve just warm or cold, cut into slices.

LIME CAKE

Freshly grated lime rind has such a wonderful aroma that I wanted to use it in a cake—I think this lime-syrup soaked cake is a great success.

1/2 cup butter
1/2 cup superfine sugar
grated rind and juice of 3 limes
2 eggs, beaten
1 1/2 cups sifted self-rising flour
3 tablespoons powdered sugar, plus extra for dusting

1. Lightly grease a 7 inch round cake pan and line the base.
2. Cream the butter and sugar together until pale and fluffy. Stir in the lime rind, then beat in the eggs a little at a time.

3. Fold in the flour, then transfer the mixture to the prepared pan. Level the surface, then make a slight dip in the center.
4. Bake in a 350°F oven for 25–30 minutes or until a skewer inserted into the center of the cake comes out clean. Leave the cake to cool in the pan.
5. Meanwhile, place the lime juice and powdered sugar in a pan over a low heat and heat gently until the powdered sugar has dissolved.
6. Prick the surface of the cake at regular intervals with a skewer and pour the syrup over the cake. Leave in the pan until cold.
7. Dust with powdered sugar to serve.

Serves 8–10
Preparation time:
25 minutes
Cooking time:
25–30 minutes
Freezing:
Recommended

DORSET APPLE CAKE

Somewhere between a cake and a scone, Dorset Apple Cake is a plain cake mixture studded with diced apple and raisins—delicious served just warm dusted with sugar.

2 cups self-rising flour
pinch of salt
1/4 cup butter
1/3 cup shortening
1/3 cup raisins
1 large cooking apple, peeled, cored and diced
1/3 cup sugar
1 egg, beaten
2 tablespoons milk
superfine sugar for dusting

Serves 8
Preparation time: 20 minutes
Cooking time: About 50 minutes
Freezing: Recommended. Thaw, then warm through in the oven

1. Sift the flour and salt into a bowl, then rub in the butter and shortening until the mixture resembles fine crumbs.
2. Stir in the raisins, apple and sugar, add the egg and milk and mix to a firm dough.
3. Press the mixture into a greased 8 inch round cake pan, levelling the surface with your fingertips.
4. Bake in a 350°F oven for about 50 minutes or until a skewer inserted into the center of the cake comes out clean. Cool on a rack.
5. Sprinkle with superfine sugar and serve warm or cold.

APPLE CIDER CAKE

½ cup butter
½ cup superfine sugar
2 eggs, beaten
1½ cups sifted self-rising flour
3 tablespoons apple cider
2 dessert apples, peeled, cored and sliced thinly
*2 tablespoons apricot Jam Glaze**
½ cup sifted powdered sugar

1. Grease an 8 inch square cake pan and line the base.
2. Cream the butter and sugar together until pale and fluffy, then beat in the eggs a little at a time. Fold in the flour and 2 tablespoons of the cider.
3. Transfer the mixture to a prepared pan. Arrange the apple slices in 4 lines, facing alternate directions, pressing down gently.
4. Bake in a 350°F oven for about 35 minutes, until risen and firm to the touch.
5. Transfer to a rack, brush with the apricot glaze and leave to cool.
6. Mix the powdered sugar with the remaining cider and brush over the cake. Leave to set, then cut into 12 squares.

Serves 12
Preparation time: 40 minutes
Cooking time: About 35 minutes
Freezing: Recommended, at end of stage 4

FRESH PEAR GINGERBREAD

Finely sliced fresh pear and chopped stem ginger make this rich gingerbread more moist than usual.

1 cup sifted all-purpose flour
1/2 cup whole wheat flour
2 teaspoons ground ginger
1 teaspoon ground cinnamon
1/2 teaspoon baking soda
2 1/2 tablespoons molasses
2 1/2 tablespoons golden syrup or light corn syrup
1/3 cup dark brown sugar, packed
1/3 cup butter
1 egg
1 tablespoon milk
1/2 lb ripe dessert pears, peeled, cored and sliced thinly
2 oz jar preserved stem ginger, chopped

Serves 12
Preparation time:
25 minutes
Cooking time:
About 50 minutes
Freezing:
Recommended

1. Grease a 6 1/2 × 3 3/4 × 3 inch loaf pan and line the base.
2. Stir the dry ingredients together in a large bowl.
3. Place the molasses, syrup, sugar and butter in a pan and heat gently, stirring, until the butter has melted.
4. Beat the egg and milk together.
5. Combine all the ingredients and stir well until evenly mixed. Transfer to the prepared pan and bake in a 325°F oven for about 50 minutes, until risen and firm to the touch. Cool on a rack.
6. Cut into slices to serve.

DATE RIPPLE LOAF

Here a date and apple puree is layered with the cake mixture to form an interesting ripple effect.

1/2 lb cooking apple, peeled and cored
1 cup pitted dates
grated rind and juice of 1 lemon
3 tablespoons apple juice or water
3/4 cup butter
3/4 cup light brown sugar, packed
3 eggs, beaten
1 1/2 cups sifted self-rising flour

1. Grease a 6 1/2 × 3 3/4 × 3 inch loaf pan and line the base.
2. Chop the apple and three-quarters of the dates and place in a saucepan with the lemon rind and juice and the apple juice or water. Cook gently, stirring, until the mixture is a soft puree. Beat well and leave to cool.

3. Cream the butter and sugar together until pale and fluffy. Gradually beat in the eggs, then fold in the flour.
4. Spread about one-third of the cake mixture over the base of the prepared pan. Top with half of the apple and date puree, spreading evenly. Repeat the layers, finishing with cake mixture.
5. Cut the remaining dates into thin slivers and arrange along the middle of the cake mixture, pressing in gently.
6. Bake in a 325°F oven for about 1¼ hours, until risen and firm to the touch; cover the surface with foil if necessary during cooking to prevent the dates from over-browning. Cool on a rack.
7. Cut into slices to serve.

Serves 12
Preparation time:
About 30 minutes
Cooking time:
About 1¼ hours
Freezing:
Recommended

FRUIT AND NUT CRUSTED CAKE

This cake stores well if wrapped in foil, sealed in a plastic bag and kept in a cool, dry place.

1 cup butter
1 cup light brown sugar, packed
4 eggs
2½ cups all-purpose flour
2 teaspoons ground mixed spice
1⅔ cups raisins
⅔ cup cut mixed peel
½ cup chopped dried apricots
4 oz jar crystallized pineapple, chopped
½ cup quartered glacé cherries
4 oz jar crystallized ginger, chopped
1 cup chopped walnuts
6 tablespoons Guinness
FOR THE TOPPING:
¼ cup walnut halves
¼ cup halved glacé cherries
⅓ cup brazil nuts
*3 tablespoons apricot Jam Glaze**

Serves about 40
Preparation time: About 1 hour
Cooking time: 3–3¼ hours
Freezing: Suitable, though unnecessary

1. Grease and line an 8 inch square cake pan with a double thickness of waxed paper.
2. Cream the butter and sugar together until pale and fluffy. Beat in the eggs one at a time.
3. Sift the flour and spice into a bowl, stir in the fruit, ginger and chopped walnuts, then fold into the creamed mixture alternately with the Guinness.
4. Transfer the mixture to the prepared pan, level the surface, then make a slight dip in the center.
5. Top with lines of walnuts, cherries and brazils.
6. Bake in a 325°F oven for 1 hour, lower the temperature to 300°F and bake for 2–2¼ hours, until a skewer inserted into the center of the cake comes out clean.
7. Transfer to a rack, brush the surface with the apricot glaze while still warm, then leave to cool.

BRAZIL NUT AND BANANA CAKE

½ cup superfine sugar
4 eggs, separated
1 cup brazil nuts, ground and toasted
1 tablespoon toasted or dried white breadcrumbs
1 tablespoon dark rum
pinch of salt
3 firm ripe bananas
⅔ cup heavy cream, whipped
1 tablespoon powdered sugar
2 teaspoons lemon juice

1. Grease an $8\frac{1}{2}$ inch springform cake pan and line the base.
2. Place three-quarters of the sugar in a bowl with the egg yolks and beat until pale. Fold in the nuts, breadcrumbs and rum.
3. Beat 3 of the egg whites with the salt until thick and foamy. Beat in the remaining sugar until stiff and glossy. Fold into the nut mixture and transfer to the prepared pan.
4. Bake in a 350°F oven for about 30 minutes, until risen and firm to the touch. Cool on a rack.
5. Meanwhile, mash 2 of the bananas and fold into the cream. Beat the remaining egg white until stiff, then beat in the powdered sugar. Fold into the banana cream.
6. Split the cake and sandwich together with half of the banana cream. Spread the remaining cream on top.
7. Slice the remaining banana, brush with the lemon juice and use to decorate the cake. Serve immediately.

Serves 8–10
Preparation time:
45 minutes
Cooking time:
About 30 minutes
Freezing:
Recommended at end of stage 4

BUTTERSCOTCH BROWNIES

These squares are moist and slightly chewy; dates or dried figs provide extra flavor.

1/2 cup butter, melted
3/4 cup dark brown sugar, packed
1 cup sifted self-rising flour
2 eggs
1/3 cup chopped walnuts
1/3 cup chopped pitted dates or dried figs (optional)

Makes 16
Preparation time: 15 minutes
Cooking time: 30–35 minutes
Freezing: Recommended

1. Grease an 8 inch square cake pan and line the base.
2. Place all the ingredients in a bowl and beat well. Transfer to the prepared pan.
3. Bake in a 350°F oven for 30–35 minutes, until just firm to the touch.
4. Cool slightly, then cut into squares. Transfer to a rack to cool completely.

BUTTERFLY CAKES

1/2 cup butter
1/2 cup superfine sugar
2 eggs, beaten
1 cup sifted self-rising flour
1/4 cup jam
2/3 cup heavy or whipping cream, whipped
powdered sugar for dusting

Makes 18–20
Preparation time: 30 minutes
Cooking time: 15–20 minutes
Freezing: Recommended; freeze uncovered until cream goes solid

1. Cream the butter and sugar together until pale and fluffy. Beat in the eggs a little at a time, then fold in the flour.
2. Divide the mixture between 18–20 paper cake cases placed in muffin pans. Bake in a 350°F oven for 15–20 minutes, until risen and firm to the touch. Cool on a rack.
3. Using a small sharp knife, remove a small circle of cake from the center of each and set aside. Place a dot of jam in each hollow and spoon or pipe a little cream on top.
4. Cut the reserved cake circles in half and replace on top of the cakes to resemble butterfly wings. Dust with powdered sugar to serve.

CANNOLI

I first tasted these delicious cheese-filled pastry tubes in New York—this is my version. You will need twelve 6 inch cannoli molds for shaping them. Serve within 1–2 hours of filling.

1 1/4 cups all-purpose flour
2 tablespoons powdered sugar
1 teaspoon cocoa powder
1 teaspoon instant coffee powder
pinch of salt
1 tablespoon butter
3 tablespoons Marsala or sweet sherry
2 tablespoons water
lightly beaten egg white
powered sugar for dusting

FOR THE FILLING:
1 1/4 cups Mascarpone or Ricotta cheese
3 tablespoons skinned and chopped pistachio nuts
1/3 cup sifted powdered sugar
3 tablespoons glacé pineapple, chopped finely
1 1/2 oz baker's semi-sweet chocolate, chopped finely

Makes 12
Preparation time: 50 minutes, plus standing time
Cooking time: 12–15 minutes
Freezing: Not recommended

1. Sift the flour, powdered sugar, cocoa, coffee and salt into a bowl. Rub in the butter. Add the Marsala or sherry and water and mix to a firm dough. Knead lightly, cover with plastic wrap and leave for 30 minutes.
2. Roll out the pastry on a lightly floured surface as thinly as possible and cut out twelve 4 inch circles.
3. Lightly grease twelve cannoli molds and wrap a piece of dough around each. Brush the edges with a little egg white to seal.
4. Deep-fry 3 or 4 cannoli at a time on their molds in hot oil for 3–4 minutes, until crisp and golden. Drain on paper towels and leave to cool. Remove from the molds and place on a rack until completely cold.
5. Meanwhile, beat together the filling ingredients. Place in a piping bag fitted with a large plain tip and carefully fill the cannoli. Dust with powdered sugar to serve.

ECCLES CAKES

3/4 lb puff pastry
2/3 cup currants
2 1/2 tablespoons cut mixed peel
2 tablespoons butter
2 tablespoons light brown granulated sugar
1/4 teaspoon ground allspice
1/4 teaspoon grated nutmeg
superfine sugar for sprinkling

1. Roll out the pastry on a floured surface to an ⅛ inch thickness and cut out twelve 4 inch circles.
2. Mix the remaining ingredients together and divide between the pastry circles.
3. Dampen the edge of each circle and fold in to encase the filling, pinching together to seal.
4. Turn the circles over and roll out to a ½ inch thickness or until the fruit is clearly visible through the pastry. Make 2 small slashes in the top of each round. Brush with water and sprinkle with superfine sugar.
5. Place on a wetted baking sheet and bake in a 425°F oven for 20–25 minutes, until crisp and golden.
6. Cool slightly on a rack; serve just warm if possible.

Makes 12
Preparation time:
30 minutes
Cooking time:
20–25 minutes
Freezing:
Recommended, at end of stage 4 if using fresh pastry

WELSH CAKES

These are a cross between scones and griddle cakes.

2¼ cups all-purpose flour
½ teaspoon baking powder
1 teaspoon grated nutmeg
¾ cup butter
⅓ cup light brown sugar, packed
½ cup mixed dried fruit
1 egg, beaten
melted butter for brushing

Makes 10–12
Preparation time: 20 minutes
Cooking time: 20–25 minutes
Freezing: Recommended. Thaw, then warm through in the oven

1. Sift the flour, baking powder and nutmeg into a bowl.
2. Rub in the butter until the mixture resembles fine crumbs, then stir in the sugar and fruit.
3. Mix to a firm dough with the egg and knead on a lightly floured surface.
4. Roll out to a ½ inch thickness and cut into 3 inch circles. Heat a griddle or large frying pan, then brush lightly with melted butter.
5. Cook the 'cakes' in 2 batches for 5–7 minutes on each side, until evenly browned and firm to the touch.
6. Cool slightly on a rack; serve warm if possible.

GEORGIAN FRUIT MUFFINS

1/2 cup butter
1/3 cup light brown sugar, packed
1 egg
1 cup self-rising flour
1 teaspoon grated nutmeg
1/2 cup mixed dried fruit
1/4 cup milk
1/4 cup sifted powdered sugar
1 tablespoon rosewater

1. Cream the butter and sugar together until pale and fluffy. Beat in the egg.
2. Sift the flour and nutmeg together, then fold into the creamed mixture.
3. Fold in the fruit and milk to give a firm dropping consistency.
4. Divide the mixture between 18 paper cases placed in muffin pans.
5. Mix the powdered sugar with the rosewater and brush carefully over the top of each muffin.
6. Bake in a 375°F oven for 15–20 minutes, until risen, golden and firm to the touch. Cool on a rack.

Makes 18
Preparation time: 25 minutes
Cooking time: 15–20 minutes
Freezing: Recommended

HONEY RUM BABAS

$^{3}/_{4}$ oz fresh yeast
$^{1}/_{3}$ cup warm milk
$1^{1}/_{2}$ cups sifted all-purpose flour
pinch of salt
$1^{1}/_{2}$ tablespoons sugar
3 eggs, beaten
$^{1}/_{3}$ cup butter
$^{1}/_{2}$ cup currants

FOR THE SYRUP:
$^{2}/_{3}$ cup honey
6 tablespoons water
3 tablespoons dark rum

TO FINISH:
*3–4 tablespoons apricot Jam Glaze**
$1^{1}/_{4}$ cups heavy cream, whipped
10 glacé cherries

Makes 10
Preparation time: 40 minutes, plus rising and cooling time
Cooking time: 15–20 minutes
Freezing: Recommended, without the cherries

1. Crumble the yeast into a bowl, add the milk and stir until well blended. Add ½ cup of the flour and mix well. Leave in a warm place for about 20 minutes until frothy.
2. Stir in the remaining ingredients and beat for 3–4 minutes.
3. Half-fill ten greased 4 inch muffin or brioche pans with the mixture. Cover with oiled plastic wrap and leave to rise in a warm place for 20 minutes, until the mixture reaches the top of the pans.
4. Bake in a 400°F oven for 15–20 minutes, until golden. Cool slightly in the pans, then turn onto a rack. Prick all over with a skewer.
5. Place the honey and water in a pan and bring to the boil. Stir in the rum. Spoon the syrup over the babas and leave until completely cold and all the syrup has been absorbed.
6. Warm the apricot glaze, brush all over the babas and leave to cool completely. Place the cream in a piping bag fitted with a star tip and pipe a whirl on to each baba. Top each with a cherry.

APPLE BUNS

These little cakes are a variation on the English rock buns, made with finely diced fresh apple instead of mixed dried fruit.

$1^{3}/_{4}$ cups all-purpose or whole wheat flour
$2^{1}/_{2}$ tablespoons ground rice
2 teaspoons baking powder
pinch of salt
$^{1}/_{3}$ cup butter
$^{1}/_{3}$ cup light brown granulated sugar
$^{1}/_{2}$ lb dessert apples, cored and diced
1 egg
2 tablespoons milk

1. Sift the dry ingredients into a large bowl; if using whole wheat flour, just stir all the dry ingredients together.
2. Rub in the butter until the mixture resembles fine crumbs, then stir in the sugar and apple.
3. Beat the egg and milk together, add to the mixture and mix to a stiff dough.
4. Divide the mixture into eight and place the mounds on a greased baking sheet. Bake in a 400°F oven for 15–20 minutes, until firm to the touch. Cool slightly on a rack. Serve warm.

Makes 8
Preparation time: About 20 minutes
Cooking time: 15–20 minutes
Freezing: Recommended. Thaw, then warm through in the oven

VARIATION

Jam Buns. Omit the apples and reduce the sugar to 1/4 cup. Divide the mixture into 8 pieces and, with floured hands, shape each into a flattened circle. Place a teaspoon of jam in the center and draw the dough around to encase the jam. Seal well. Place seam side down on a greased baking sheet and bake as above.

JAPONAIS

Based on a meringue mixture, these small, slightly chewy cakes have ground nuts added to them.

1 cup ground almonds
3 egg whites
1 teaspoon lemon juice
1/4 teaspoon almond extract
2/3 cup superfine sugar
1 tablespoon cornstarch
*3/4 quantity coffee Creme au Beurre**
12 chocolate-coated coffee beans

Makes 12
Preparation time: About 1 hour
Cooking time: 40 minutes
Freezing: Recommended

1. Grease a 13 × 9 inch jelly roll pan or baking sheet and line with waxed paper.
2. Place the ground almonds in a non-stick frying pan and cook, stirring frequently, until golden. Leave to cool.
3. Beat the egg whites until stiff, then beat in the lemon juice and almond extract. Beat in the sugar a tablespoon at a time; stir the cornstarch into the last tablespoon of sugar and fold in. Fold in the ground almonds.
4. Spread the mixture evenly in the prepared pan. Bake in a 325°F oven for 30 minutes.
5. Cool slightly, then invert onto a large board. Cut out twenty-four 2 inch circles and leave until cold.
6. Roughly crush the trimmings, place on the baking sheet and return to the oven for 10 minutes. Leave until cold, then crush to fine crumbs.
7. Sandwich the circles together in pairs with a third of the creme au beurre. Use the rest to cover completely.
8. Dip in the crumbs to coat evenly. Neaten the shapes and press a chocolate coffee bean into the center of each.

SPICY JELLY DOUGHNUTS

Generously spiced dough is the basis for these doughnuts; use jelly of your choice in the center.

1/4 oz fresh yeast
2 tablespoons light brown sugar
2/3 cup milk, warmed
2 cups all-purpose flour
1/2 teaspoon ground allspice
1/2 teaspoon ground cinnamon
1/4 teaspoon ground cloves
1/4 teaspoon grated nutmeg
2 tablespoons butter
about 8 teaspoons jam
superfine sugar for coating

1. Mix the yeast, sugar, milk and ½ cup of the flour together. Leave in a warm place for about 10–15 minutes, until frothy.
2. Meanwhile, sift the remaining flour with the spices. Rub in the butter, then mix to a soft dough with the yeast liquid.
3. Knead on a lightly floured surface, then place in a bowl, cover with oiled plastic wrap and leave to rise in a warm place for about 45 minutes to 1 hour, until doubled in size.
4. Knead lightly, then divide into 16 pieces. With floured hands, flatten each piece of dough, then place about ½ teaspoon jelly in the center. Draw the dough around the jelly to encase it and reshape into a ball.
5. Place the dough balls well apart on a greased baking sheet, cover with oiled plastic wrap and leave to rise in a warm place for about 30 minutes, until doubled in size.
6. Deep-fry the doughnuts four at a time in hot oil for 4–5 minutes, turning frequently, until golden. Drain on paper towels, then roll in superfine sugar. Serve warm.

Makes 16
Preparation time:
45 minutes, plus rising time
Cooking time:
16–20 minutes
Freezing:
Not recommended

RHUBARB STRUDEL

Rhubarb makes a refreshing change in this classic pastry.

2 cups all-purpose flour
pinch of salt
1 egg, beaten
1/3 cup warm water
2 tablespoons sunflower oil
FOR THE FILLING:
1/2 cup butter
1 1/2 cups fresh white breadcrumbs
1 lb prepared rhubard, cut into 1/4 inch slices
1/2 cup chopped cashew nuts, toasted
1/3 cup golden raisins
1/3 cup light brown granulated sugar
1 tablespoon ground cinnamon
powdered sugar for dusting

Serves 8
Preparation time: About 45 minutes, plus standing time
Cooking time: 35–40 minutes
Freezing: Not recommended

1. Sift the flour and salt into a bowl. Beat the egg, water and oil together and add to the bowl. Mix together with your fingertips until a smooth dough forms.
2. Knead the dough on a floured surface for 2–3 minutes, then cover in plastic wrap and leave for 30 minutes.
3. Meanwhile, prepare the filling. Set half of the butter aside; melt the other half in a pan, add the breadcrumbs and fry until crisp and golden. Place in a bowl and stir in the rhubarb, nuts, golden raisins, sugar and cinnamon.
4. Roll out the pastry as thinly as possible on a clean floured dish cloth to a 24 × 16 inch rectangle. Trim the edges with a sharp knife.
5. Melt the remaining butter and use to brush the pastry. Sprinkle with the filling to within 1 inch of the edges. Fold in the 2 short sides.
6. Using the dish cloth, roll the strudel, from a long side, to encase the filling. Seal the edge with water.
7. Carefully transfer the strudel to a baking sheet, shaping it into a crescent if necessary. Brush with the remaining butter and bake in a 350°F oven for 35–40 minutes, until crisp and golden.
8. Cool slightly on a baking sheet, then dust with powdered sugar and cut into slices. Serve warm.

VARIATION

Apple. Substitute 1 lb thinly sliced cooking apples for the rhubarb, and use filberts instead of cashew nuts.

PANFORTE

Panforte is a speciality of Siena in Tuscany. It will keep for several weeks in an airtight container.

1 cup whole unblanched almonds
$1^2/_3$ cups chopped mixed candied fruit; use at least $^2/_3$ cup orange and $^1/_2$ cup lemon
$^1/_2$ cup sifted all-purpose flour
$^1/_4$ teaspoon each ground cinnamon, cloves and coriander
$^1/_4$ teaspoon grated nutmeg
$^1/_2$ cup superfine sugar
2 tablespoons honey
2 tablespoons water
powdered sugar for dusting

Serves 12
Preparation time:
About 40 minutes
Cooking time:
30–35 minutes
Freezing:
Not recommended

1. Grease an 8 inch loose-bottomed round cake pan and line the base with rice paper.
2. Place the almonds, candied fruit, flour and spices in a bowl and mix well.
3. Place the sugar, honey and water in a saucepan and heat gently until the sugar has dissolved. Bring to the boil and boil until it reaches 220°F on a candy thermometer or until 2 chilled spoons will stick together when dipped in the mixture. Pour onto the dry ingredients; mix well.
4. Press the mixture into the prepared pan.
5. Bake in a 325°F oven for 30–35 minutes, until the surface of the mixture has bubbled evenly. Trim the edges and leave in the pan to cool.
6. Remove from the pan but leave on the base until completely cold, then transfer to a serving plate. Dust with powdered sugar and cut into small wedges to serve.

POPPY SEED LATTICE CAKE

This cake is based on one I tried in West Berlin.

2 cups self-rising flour
pinch of salt
$^1/_3$ cup butter
$^1/_3$ cup superfine sugar
2 eggs, beaten
2 tablespoons apricot Jam Glaze, warmed*
FOR THE FILLING:
$^1/_4$ cup milk
$^1/_4$ cup ground poppy seeds
$^1/_4$ cup golden raisins
$^1/_4$ cup currants
$2^1/_2$ tablespoons cut mixed peel
$^1/_4$ cup slivered almonds, toasted
$^1/_4$ cup superfine sugar
1 egg, beaten

1. Grease an 8 inch square cake pan and line the base.
2. First prepare the filling. Place the milk in a small saucepan and bring to the boil. Stir in the poppy seeds, then simmer gently, stirring, for 1–2 minutes, until the milk is completely absorbed. Remove from the heat and stir in the remaining ingredients. Set aside.
3. Sift the flour and salt into a bowl, then rub in the butter until the mixture resembles fine crumbs. Stir in the sugar, then mix to a firm dough with the eggs.
4. Spread about three-quarters of the cake mixture evenly over the base of the prepared pan. Spread the filling over the top.
5. Place the remaining cake mixture in a piping bag fitted with a 1/4 inch plain tip and pipe a lattice over the filling.
6. Bake in a 350°F oven for 30–35 minutes, until risen and firm to the touch.
7. Transfer to a rack, brush the top with the apricot glaze, then leave to cool. Cut into squares to serve.

Serves 12–16
Preparation time:
40 minutes
Cooking time:
30–35 minutes
Freezing:
Recommended, at end of stage 6. Thaw, warm and glaze to serve.

NORWEGIAN APRICOT SPONGE CAKE

This gateau is best made and left in a cool place for several hours before serving. For an extra special flavor, sprinkle the sponge layers with a little apricot brandy before sandwiching them together.

2 × 15 oz cans apricot halves in fruit juice, drained
*1 quantity Creme au Beurre**
1¼ cups heavy cream, lightly whipped
2 × 8 inch Sponge Cakes, unfilled (see page 8)
½ cup slivered almonds, toasted

Serves 12–16
Preparation time: 45 minutes, plus making the sponge cakes
Freezing: Recommended; freeze uncovered until solid

1. Set aside 4 apricot halves for decoration. Puree the rest in a blender or food processor. Beat into the creme au beurre, then fold in the cream.
2. Split each sponge cake in half horizontally and sandwich together using about half of the apricot cream.
3. Spread just under half of the remaining filling over the side of the cake, then press on the almonds.
4. Transfer the cake to a serving plate and cover the top with half of the remaining filling. Spoon the rest into a piping bag fitted with a large plain tip and pipe large dots around the edge of the cake.
5. Cut the reserved apricot halves into segments and use to decorate the cake.

DATE AND ORANGE TORTE

I love the combination of date and walnut, and I've used it here with orange to make my variation of a classic Austrian recipe.

1 cup all-purpose flour
pinch of salt
⅓ cup sweet butter
1½ tablespoons superfine sugar
2 teaspoons cold water
FOR THE FILLING AND TOPPING:
4 egg whites
¾ cup superfine sugar
1⅓ cups chopped dates
1 cup chopped walnuts
⅓ cup cut mixed peel
finely grated rind of 1 large orange
⅔ cup heavy cream, whipped
julienne strips of orange rind to decorate

1. Sift the flour and salt into a bowl, then rub in the butter until the mixture resembles fine crumbs. Stir in the sugar and mix to a firm dough with the water.
2. Press the pastry over the base of a greased 8½ inch springform cake pan and prick very well. Bake in a 350°F oven for 20 minutes.
3. Meanwhile, beat the egg whites until stiff, then beat in the sugar a tablespoon at a time, until stiff and glossy. Fold in the dates, walnuts, peel and orange rind and spread over the pastry base. Return to the oven for 1 hour. Leave in the pan until cold.
4. Spread the cream over the surface of the cake and decorate with the orange rind.

Serves 12
Preparation time:
45 minutes
Cooking time:
1 hour 20 minutes
Freezing:
Recommended; freeze uncovered until solid

AUSTRALIAN FRUIT AND NUT CAKE

This is a really chunky fruit cake—fruit and nuts held together with the minimum of cake mixture. It keeps well in a cool, dry place if wrapped in foil and sealed in a plastic bag.

1 cup mixed green and red glacé cherries
1/3 cup cut mixed peel
2/3 cup raisins
1 cup chopped dates
1/3 cup dark rum
finely grated rind of 1 lemon
1 cup roughly chopped walnuts
1/2 cup unblanched whole almonds
1/2 cup brazil nuts
1 cup all-purpose flour
1/2 cup superfine sugar
1/2 teaspoon baking powder
pinch of salt
3 eggs, beaten

Serves 20
Preparation time: 25 minutes, plus soaking time
Cooking time: About 1¼ hours
Freezing: Suitable, though unnecessary

1. Grease and line a 7 inch round cake pan.
2. Place the cherries, peel, raisins, dates and rum in a bowl and leave to soak for at least 30 minutes; it can be left to soak for several hours. Drain, reserving the rum.
3. Place the drained fruits, lemon rind and nuts in a large bowl. Sift the dry ingredients together and stir into the fruit mixture. Add the eggs and mix well.
4. Transfer to the prepared pan and bake in a 300°F oven for about 1¼ hours or until a skewer inserted into the center of the cake comes out clean.
5. Spoon the reserved rum over the top of the cake immediately and leave in the pan for 5 minutes. Transfer to a rack to cool. Cut into thin slices to serve.

HONEY BAKLAVA

A classic Greek pastry made with the traditional paper-thin filo pastry, lots of nuts and plenty of spice.

1/2 lb filo pastry
about 3/4 cup sweet butter, melted
1 2/3 cups chopped mixed nuts, e.g. walnuts, almonds, peanuts, pine nuts
1/3 cup superfine sugar
1 tablespoon ground cinnamon
1 teaspoon grated nutmeg
2/3 cup honey
1 tablespoon lemon juice

1. Brush a 9 × 12 inch deep baking pan with melted butter. Layer 4 sheets of filo pastry in the pan, folding the edges under to fit and brushing each sheet generously with melted butter.
2. Set aside another 4 sheets of filo pastry for the top. Divide the remaining sheets into 2 equal piles. Keep the pastry covered with a clean, dampened dishcloth to prevent it drying out.
3. Mix the nuts, sugar and spices together and sprinkle a third over the pastry in the pan.
4. Place one of the piles of filo pastry on top, brushing each pastry layer with melted butter.
5. Cover with another third of the nut mixture, then the other pile of pastry, brushing each layer with butter. Sprinkle the remaining nuts on top.
6. Cover with the reserved 4 sheets of pastry, brushing between each layer with butter.
7. Cut through the top pastry lengthways in 3 evenly spaced lines, then cut across diagonally to get diamond shapes; you should have 12 perfect diamond shapes.
8. Sprinkle with 1 tablespoon cold water and bake in a 350°F oven for about 40 minutes, until crisp and golden.
9. Warm the honey and lemon juice together and pour over the warm pastry. Leave until cold, then cut through.

Serves 12
Preparation time:
25–30 minutes
Cooking time:
About 40 minutes
Freezing:
Recommended

WALNUT AND ZUCCHINI CAKE

It may seem strange to add a vegetable to a cake but zucchini produces a moist texture which goes well with the crunchiness of walnuts in this recipe. Carrots may be used in place of the zucchini for an equally delicious carrot cake.

2 cups grated zucchini
1 cup sunflower oil
3/4 cup light brown sugar, packed
3/4 cup superfine sugar
4 eggs
1 cup whole wheat flour
1 cup sifted all-purpose flour
1 teaspoon baking soda
1/2 teaspoon salt
1/2 teaspoon ground allspice
1 teaspoon ground cinnamon
1/4 teaspoon grated nutmeg
3 small oranges
1 cup chopped walnuts
grated rind of 1 lemon, and 2 teaspoons juice
*1 1/2 quantities Creme au Beurre**
apple mint or other fresh herbs to decorate

Serves 16
Preparation time: About 1 hour
Cooking time: 45 minutes
Freezing: Recommended, at end of stage 10

1. Grease two 9 inch round cake pans and line the bases.
2. Place the zucchini in a clean dish cloth and squeeze out excess liquid.
3. Place the oil and sugars in a bowl and beat well. Add the eggs and continue beating until pale.
4. Mix the dry ingredients together.
5. Grate the rind from the oranges. Stir the zucchini, half of the orange rind and the walnuts into the egg mixture. Fold in the dry ingredients, then transfer to the prepared pans.
6. Bake in a 350°F oven for about 45 minutes, until risen and firm to the touch. Transfer to a rack to cool.
7. Add the remaining orange rind, 2 tablespoons juice from one of the oranges, the lemon rind and lemon juice to the creme au beurre and beat well.
8. Remove pith from 2 remaining oranges with a sharp knife, slice the flesh, then cut each slice into quarters.
9. Split each cake in half horizontally, then sandwich all 4 layers together with half of the creme au beurre.
10. Transfer the cake to a serving plate and cover the top and side with the remaining creme au beurre.
11. Decorate with the orange pieces and herbs.

ANISEED AND LEMON KUGELHUPF

This light, spongy yeast cake is best served just warm with butter, but it is also delicious sliced and toasted.

1 envelope easy blend yeast
2 cups sifted all-purpose flour
1/4 cup superfine sugar
1/2 teaspoon salt
finely grated rind of 1/2 lemon
1 tablespoon aniseed
1/3 cup cut mixed peel
3 tablespoons warm water
1/2 cup butter, melted
3 eggs, beaten
powdered sugar for dusting

Serves 16
Preparation time: About 20 minutes, plus rising time
Cooking time: About 30 minutes
Freezing: Recommended

1. Place the yeast, flour, sugar, salt, lemon rind, aniseed and mixed peel in a large bowl and mix well.
2. Add the water, butter and eggs and beat for 2 minutes.
3. Cover the bowl with plastic wrap and leave to rise in a warm place for 1–2 hours, until doubled in size.
4. Stir the mixture to ensure that the ingredients are evenly mixed, then transfer to a greased 8 inch Kugelhupf mold or a 9–9½ inch ring mold. Cover with plastic wrap and leave in a warm place for 1–2 hours, until the mixture is almost level with the top of the pan.
5. Remove the plastic wrap and bake in a 400°F oven for about 30 minutes, until risen and golden, and the base of the cake sounds hollow when tapped with your knuckle. Cool on a rack.
6. Dust with powdered sugar and serve just warm with butter.

GENOA FRUIT CAKE

My favorite sort of fruit cake—rich in fruit but not too dark or bitter. It keeps well in a cool, dry place if wrapped in foil and sealed in a plastic bag.

3/4 cup butter
3/4 cup light brown granulated sugar
1/3 cup golden syrup or 2½ tablespoons each light corn syrup and molasses
3 eggs
1 cup currants
1⅔ cups golden raisins
1¼ cups raisins
1 cup cut mixed peel
1/4 cup quartered glacé cherries
1 cup ground almonds
2¼ cups all-purpose flour
1 teaspoon baking powder
2/3 cup milk
1/4 cup rum, whisky or brandy (optional)

1. Grease and line a 9 inch round cake pan with a double thickness of waxed paper.
2. Cream the butter, sugar and syrup together until pale and fluffy. Beat in the eggs one at a time.
3. Mix all the dried fruits, peel and cherries together.
4. Sift the ground almonds, flour and baking powder together. Stir in the fruit, then fold into the creamed mixture with the milk.
5. Transfer the mixture to the prepared pan and bake in a 225°F oven for about 4 hours, until a skewer inserted into the center of the cake comes out clean. Leave in the pan to cool.
6. If you wish, when almost cold, prick the surface of the cake with a skewer and pour over the rum, whisky or brandy until absorbed.

Serves 16–20
Preparation time:
25 minutes
Cooking time:
About 4 hours
Freezing:
Suitable, though unnecessary

GERMAN RUM 'TREE' CAKE

The time it takes to make this cake may be daunting, but it really is worth all the effort for a special occasion. It gets its name from the fact that the layers look like the inner rings of a tree when cut.

*14 oz Almond Paste**
6 tablespoons whipping cream
1 1/4 cups sweet butter
1 cup all-purpose flour
1/2 cup cornstarch
1/4 cup rum
1 teaspoon finely grated lemon or orange rind
10 eggs, separated
3/4 cups superfine sugar
pinch of salt
1 1/2 cups plum jam, warmed and sieved
3/4 cup ground pistachio nuts
1 tablespoon golden or corn syrup
3 1/2 oz baker's semi-sweet chocolate, broken into pieces

Serves 20–24
Preparation and cooking time: About 2 1/2 hours, plus chilling
Freezing: Recommended

1. Grease and flour a 9 1/2 inch springform cake pan and line the base with waxed paper.
2. Beat the almond paste and cream together until light and fluffy.
3. Beat 1 cup of the butter until soft, then sift in the flours and stir in half of the rum and the lemon or orange rind. Stir in the almond paste mixture.
4. Beat the egg yolks and half of the sugar together until pale and thick enough for the beater to leave a trail. Fold into the cake mixture.
5. Beat the egg whites until soft peaks form, then beat in the remaining sugar a tablespoon at a time. Fold into the cake mixture.
6. Spread 4 tablespoons of the mixture over the base of the prepared pan with a palette knife or pastry brush. Broil for 2–3 minutes, until golden and just firm to the touch. Repeat the process.
7. Brush with jam and sprinkle with 1–2 teaspoons of the pistachios. Spread and cook 2 more layers as before, then brush with jam and sprinkle with pistachios.
8. Repeat these layers until all the cake mixture is used up; you will have some nuts and jam left over.
9. Leave the cake in the pan to cool, then chill overnight.
10. Place the cake on a rack over a plastic tray. Brush the top and side with warmed plum jam.
11. Place the remaining butter and rum in a saucepan with the syrup. Bring just to the boil, then remove from the heat and add the chocolate, stirring until melted.

12. Cool this mixture until it is thick enough to coat the back of a wooden spoon, then pour it over the cake, tapping the rack against the plastic tray if necessary to ensure that the icing flows and coats the cake evenly.
13. Sprinkle the remaining pistachios over the surface of the cake in the design of a tree. Leaving until the icing has completely set before transferring the cake to a serving plate. Cut into thin slices to serve.

BANANA COCONUT CHEESECAKE

Banana and coconut go well together—and this crisp coconut base topped with a banana cheese mixture is no exception. Eat on the day it is made or the banana will discolor.

1 cup self-rising flour
pinch of salt
1/3 cup butter
2/3 cup flaked coconut
3 tablespoons superfine sugar
1 egg yolk

FOR THE FILLING:
1/3 cup superfine sugar
1 1/2 cups cream cheese
4 ripe bananas
juice of 1 large lemon
1 envelope gelatin, soaked in 2 tablespoons water
2/3 cup heavy cream, lightly whipped

Serves 8–10
Preparation time: 30 minutes
Cooking time: 20–25 minutes
Setting time: 4–6 hours
Freezing: Recommended, at end of stage 6; freeze uncovered until solid

1. Grease an 8½ inch springform pan and line the side with waxed paper.
2. Sift the flour and salt into a bowl, then rub in the butter until the mixture resembles fine crumbs. Stir in the coconut and sugar, then add the egg yolk and mix to a firm dough.
3. Press the mixture evenly over the base of the prepared pan and prick well. Bake in a 375°F oven for 20–25 minutes until golden. Leave to cool in the pan.
4. Meanwhile, prepare the filling. Beat together the sugar and cheese.
5. Roughly mash 3 of the bananas with all but 1 teaspoon of the lemon juice. Stir in the cheese mixture.
6. Heat the gelatin gently until dissolved. Stir in a little of the banana mixture, then fold into the remaining mixture. Fold in the cream, then pour onto the prepared base. Chill for 4–6 hours, until set.
7. Unmold onto a serving plate. Slice the remaining banana, brush with the remaining lemon juice and use to decorate the cheesecake.

BLUEBERRY CHEESECAKE

4 cups crushed gingersnaps
1/3 cup butter, melted
1 cup curd or farmer's cheese
1/3 cup light brown sugar, packed
2 eggs, separated
5 oz baker's semi-sweet chocolate, melted
2 × 8 oz cans blueberries in fruit juice
2 teaspoons gelatin
2/3 cup whipping cream, lightly whipped

Serves 8–10
Preparation time: About 45 minutes
Setting time: 4–6 hours
Freezing: Recommended; freeze uncovered until solid

1. Line the side of an 8 inch springform pan with waxed paper.
2. Mix together the crushed gingersnaps and butter and press firmly and evenly over the base of the pan. Chill while preparing the filling.
3. Beat together the cheese, two-thirds of the sugar, the egg yolks and all but about 2 tablespoons of the chocolate.
4. Drain the blueberries and set aside; reserve 3 tablespoons of the juice. Soak the gelatin in the reserved juice until softened, then heat gently until dissolved. Stir in a little of the cheese mixture, then fold into the remaining mixture.
5. Beat the egg whites until stiff, then beat in the remaining sugar. Fold the cream and then the egg whites into the cheese mixture.
6. Arrange the blueberries over the base, then pour the cheese mixture on top.
7. Remelt the remaining chocolate if necessary and, using a teaspoon, drizzle it over the top of the cheesecake. Using a skewer, swirl the chocolate to give a pattern. Chill for 4–6 hours, until set. Unmold onto a plate to serve.

FILBERT AND CHERRY CHEESECAKE

This is an unusual baked cheesecake, made very moist with ground filberts, semolina and cherries.

15 oz can cherries in syrup
1/4 cup butter
3/4 cup curd or farmer's cheese
1/3 cup superfine sugar
3 eggs, separated
1 cup ground filberts, browned (see page 70)
1 tablespoon semolina
2 tablespoons cherry or other red jam

1. Drain the cherries, reserving 1 tablespoon of the syrup. Pit them and leave on paper towels to drain.

2. Cream the butter, cheese and sugar together until smooth. Beat in the egg yolks.
3. Mix the filberts and semolina together, then fold into the creamed mixture. Fold in the cherries.
4. Beat the egg whites until stiff, then fold into the mixture. Transfer to a greased and floured 8½ inch springform pan and bake in a 350°F oven for about 45 minutes, until risen, golden and just firm to the touch. Cool on a rack.
5. Place the jam and reserved cherry juice in a pan and bring to the boil. Strain and brush over the surface of the cake. Leave until set, then transfer to a serving plate.

Serves 8–10
Preparation time:
About 40 minutes
Cooking time:
About 45 minutes
Freezing:
Recommended; freeze uncovered until solid

GINGER AND ALMOND CHEESECAKE

3 cups crushed graham crackers or gingersnaps
1/3 cup butter, melted
1 teaspoon ground cinnamon
1/4 cup honey
2 eggs
grated rind and juice of 1/2 lemon
pinch of salt
1 tablespoon cornstarch
1/2 cup whipping cream
1 cup sieved cottage cheese
2 oz jar preserved stem ginger, chopped
1/4 cup chopped blanched almonds

Serves 8–10
Preparation time:
45 minutes
Cooking time:
About 40 minutes
Freezing:
Not recommended

1. Mix together the crumbs, butter and cinnamon. Press all except 2 tablespoons onto the base and side of an 8 inch round cake pan. Chill while preparing the filling.
2. Beat together the honey, egg, lemon rind and juice, salt, cornstarch, cream and cottage cheese.
3. Sprinkle the stem ginger over the base, then pour the cheese mixture on top.
4. Mix the almonds with the reserved crumbs and sprinkle over the surface of the cheesecake.
5. Bake in a 350°F oven for about 40 minutes, until just set. Leave in the pan to cool, then transfer to a serving plate.

ORANGE AND LEMON CHEESECAKE

3 cups crushed graham crackers
1/3 cup butter, melted
2 cups low fat Ricotta cheese
2/3 cup sour cream
1/2 cup superfine sugar
1 teaspoon each grated orange and lemon rind
1/4 cup cut mixed peel
3 eggs, separated
36 whole blanched almonds to decorate (optional)

1. Line the side of an 8½ inch springform pan with waxed paper.
2. Mix together the crumbs and butter and press over the base of the pan. Chill while preparing the filling.
3. Beat together the cheese, sour cream, half of the sugar, the orange and lemon rind, peel and egg yolks.
4. Beat the egg whites until stiff, then beat in the remaining sugar a little at a time. Fold into the cheese mixture. Transfer to the prepared pan and arrange the almonds decoratively around the edge if you wish.
5. Bake in a 350°F oven for about 45 minutes, until golden and just firm. Leave to cool in the pan, then transfer to a serving plate.

Serves 8–10
Preparation time: About 30 minutes
Cooking time: About 45 minutes
Freezing: Recommended; freeze uncovered until solid

SUMMER FRUIT CHEESECAKE

This is a quick and easy cheesecake to make as it relies on a flavored yogurt as one of its main ingredients.

3/4 cup all-purpose flour
1/4 cup butter
2 tablespoons superfine sugar
2 cups redcurrants
1/4 cup granulated sugar
2/3 cup whipping cream
1 3/4 cups strawberry yogurt
1 envelope gelatin, soaked in 2 tablespoons water
2 egg whites
redcurrants or strawberries to decorate

Serves 8–10
Preparation time: 25 minutes, plus chilling
Cooking time: 20–25 minutes
Setting time: 4–6 hours
Freezing: Recommended, at end of stage 7; freeze uncovered until solid

1. Line the side of an 8 inch springform pan with waxed paper. Lightly grease the base of the pan.
2. Sift the flour into the bowl, rub in the butter until the mixture resembles fine crumbs, then stir in the superfine sugar. Knead the mixture to form a firm dough, then press evenly over the base of the pan and prick well with a fork.
3. Bake in a 350°F oven for 20–25 minutes, until golden. Leave to cool in the pan.
4. Meanwhile, place the redcurrants and granulated sugar in a pan and simmer until just soft. Leave to cool.
5. Place the redcurrants, cream and yogurt in a large bowl and mix well.
6. Heat the gelatin gently until dissolved. Stir in a little of the cheesecake mixture, then fold into the remaining mixture. Chill for 10–15 minutes until just on the point of setting.
7. Beat the egg whites until stiff, then fold into the cheesecake mixture. Spoon over the prepared base and chill for 4–6 hours, until set.
8. Unmold the cheesecake onto a serving plate and decorate with redcurrants or strawberries to serve.

DEEP-PAN CHEESECAKE

3 cups crushed graham crackers
1/3 cup butter, melted
4 cups cream cheese
3/4 cup superfine sugar
4 eggs
1/2 cup sifted all-purpose flour
1 1/4 cups plain yogurt
grated rind of 1 lemon
1/3 cup quartered glacé cherries
1/3 cup currants

1. Grease the side of a 9½ inch springform pan.
2. Mix together the cracker crumbs and butter and press onto the base of the pan. Chill while preparing the filling.
3. Beat together the cheese, sugar, eggs, flour, yogurt and lemon rind until smooth.
4. Sprinkle the cherries and currants over the base, then pour over the cheese mixture.
5. Bake in a 350°F oven for about 50 minutes, until just set. Switch off the oven, but leave the cake in the oven until cold.
6. Remove from the pan and transfer to a serving plate.

Serves 12–16
Preparation time:
25 minutes
Cooking time:
About 50 minutes
Freezing:
Recommended; freeze uncovered until solid

GATEAU GANACHE

8 inch chocolate Sponge Cake, unfilled (see page 8)
*1 quantity Chocolate Ganache**
2/3 cup heavy cream, whipped
powdered sugar for dusting
10–12 chocolates to decorate

Serves 10–12
Preparation time: 40 minutes, plus making sponge cake
Freezing: Recommended, without chocolates. Freeze uncovered until solid

1. Cut the sponge cake horizontally into 3 layers.
2. Spread each of the bottom 2 layers with a third of the ganache, then half of the cream.
3. Sandwich the layers together, then dust the top layer with sifted powdered sugar.
4. Fill a piping bag fitted with a star tip with the remaining ganache and pipe 10–12 rosettes around the top of the cake. Decorate with chocolates.

STRAWBERRY GATEAU

Serve this gateau the day it is made.

8 inch Sponge Cake, unfilled (see page 8)
*1/2 cup strawberry Jam Glaze**
1 2/3 cups sliced strawberries
2/3 cup heavy cream, whipped
1/4 cup slivered almonds, toasted

Serves 8–10
Preparation time: 30 minutes, plus making sponge cake
Freezing: Not recommended

1. Split the cake in half horizontally and spread each cut side with 2 tablespoons strawberry glaze.
2. Roughly chop the end pieces of the strawberries and stir into the cream. Spread this over the base layer of sponge cake. Top with the remaining layer.
3. Arrange the strawberry slices decoratively over the top of the cake in circles.
4. Brush the remaining glaze carefully over the fruit and the side of the cake.
5. Press the slivered almonds onto the side.

ALMOND LAYER CAKE

5 eggs, separated
$\frac{2}{3}$ cup superfine sugar
1 teaspoon finely grated lemon rind
1 tablespoon lemon juice
1 tablespoon hot water
$\frac{1}{3}$ cup ground rice
1 cup ground almonds
$\frac{1}{4}$ cup slivered almonds
*1 quantity Frangipane Cream**
powdered sugar for dusting

Serves 10–12
Preparation time: 40 minutes
Cooking time: About 40 minutes
Freezing: Recommended

1. Grease an $8\frac{1}{2}$ inch springform cake pan and line the base.
2. Place the egg yolks, sugar, lemon rind and juice, and water in a bowl and beat for about 10 minutes, until pale and thick. Fold in the ground rice and ground almonds.
3. Beat the egg whites until stiff then fold into the mixture. Transfer to the prepared pan, sprinkle with the slivered almonds and bake in a 350°F oven for about 40 minutes, until risen and firm to the touch. Cool on a rack.
4. Cut the cake horizontally into 3 layers and sandwich together with the frangipane cream. Dust with powdered sugar and serve with raspberries, strawberries or cherries.

BRANDY SNAP BASKET GATEAU

Brandy snaps have a wonderful crisp texture which contrasts well with the soft cake and whipped cream.

2 tablespoons butter
2 tablespoons superfine sugar
1 tablespoon golden syrup or 1/2 tablespoon each light corn syrup and molasses
1/4 cup all-purpose flour
1/2 teaspoon ground ginger
3 large pieces preserved stem ginger
8 inch Sponge Cake, unfilled (see page 8), flavored with 2 teaspoons ground ginger (added with flour)
1 1/4 cups heavy cream, lightly whipped

Serves 12
Preparation time: About 50 minutes, plus making sponge cake
Cooking time: About 20 minutes
Freezing: Not recommended

1. Line 2 baking sheets with waxed paper.
2. Place the butter, sugar and syrup in a pan and heat gently until the butter has melted. Sift in the flour and ginger and mix well.
3. Spoon 3 three-quarter teaspoons of the mixture onto each baking sheet, spacing them well apart. Bake one sheet at a time, in a 350°F oven for about 4 minutes, until golden.
4. Leave to cool slightly, then press each brandy snap over an inverted egg cup—about 1 1/2 inch diameter—and leave until cold and brittle.
5. Repeat the process to make another 6 'baskets'.
6. Spoon the remaining mixture onto a baking sheet and bake for 5–6 minutes until golden. Leave until cold, then crush roughly.
7. Cut one piece of ginger into 12 pieces, and finely chop the other 2 pieces.
8. Split the sponge cake in half horizontally. Cover one half with about a quarter of the cream and sprinkle with the chopped ginger.
9. Sandwich the two halves of cake together and place on a flat plate. Cover the top and side with about two-thirds of the remaining cream. Press the brandy snap crumbs onto the side to coat evenly.
10. Place the remaining cream in a piping bag fitted with a star tip.
11. Arrange the 12 brandy snap baskets around the top edge of the cake. Pipe a whirl of cream into each and top with a piece of stem ginger.

PINEAPPLE NUT MERINGUE GATEAU

½ cup butter
½ cup superfine sugar
4 extra large egg yolks
2 tablespoons milk
1 cup all-purpose flour
1 teaspoon baking powder
FOR THE MERINGUE:
4 extra large egg whites
pinch of salt
¾ cup superfine sugar
½ cup grated or chopped filberts
½ teaspoon ground cinnamon
FOR THE FILLING:
16 oz can pineapple pieces in natural juice, drained
1 cup heavy cream, whipped

Serves 12
Preparation time: About 45 minutes
Cooking time: About 55 minutes
Freezing: Recommended, at end of stage 6

1. Grease two 8½ inch springform pans or round loose-bottomed cake pans and line the bases.
2. Cream the butter and sugar together until pale and fluffy. Beat in the egg yolks and milk.
3. Sift flour and baking powder together, then fold into the creamed mixture. Divide between the prepared pans.
4. For the meringue, beat the egg whites with the salt until stiff, then beat in all but 2 teaspoons of the sugar, a tablespoon at a time. Divide the meringue between the pans, spreading over the cake mixture. Sprinkle with the filberts.
5. Mix the cinnamon and remaining sugar together and sprinkle over the filberts.
6. Bake in a 350°F oven for about 55 minutes, until crisp and golden. Carefully transfer to a rack to cool.
7. To assemble the gateau, roughly chop the pineapple and fold into the cream. Place one cake, meringue side down, on a serving plate, spread with the pineapple cream and top with the second cake, meringue side up.

COCONUT AND MANGO LAYER

If you wish to decorate this tropical cake, pipe whirls of cream on top and trim with pieces of mango.

8 inch Sponge Cake, unfilled (see page 8)
1 cup milk
1 cup unsweetened flaked coconut
3 egg yolks
¼ cup superfine sugar
2 teaspoons gelatin soaked in ⅓ cup sweet white wine
1 mango, peeled and diced
powdered sugar for dusting

1. Line the side of an 8 inch springform pan with waxed paper.
2. Cut the cake in half horizontally and carefully place the base in the pan.
3. Place the milk and coconut in a pan and heat gently; strain.
4. Beat the egg yolks and sugar together until pale, then stir in the coconut milk. Return to the pan and cook very gently, stirring, until thickened; do not allow to boil.
5. Heat the gelatin gently until dissolved, then stir into the coconut mixture. Leave to cool, then stir in the mango. Pour over the sponge cake base and carefully cover with the top layer. Chill for 2–3 hours until set.
6. Unmold and dust with powdered sugar to serve.

Serves 10
Preparation time:
30 minutes, plus making sponge cake
Setting time:
2–3 hours
Freezing:
Recommended

LEMON GATEAU

3 eggs
2/3 cup superfine sugar
2 tablespoons butter, melted
grated rind and juice of 2 lemons
2/3 cup all-purpose flour
1 tablespoon cornstarch
2 tablespoons water
1/2 cup lemon curd
1 1/4 cups heavy cream, whipped
1/4 cup finely chopped pistachios
1 1/2 lemon slices to decorate

Serves 10–12
Preparation time: 45–50 minutes
Cooking time: About 15 minutes
Freezing: Recommended without lemon triangles; freeze uncovered until solid

1. Grease three 8 inch round cake pans and line the bases.
2. Place the eggs and just over half of the sugar in a bowl over a pan of simmering water and beat, using a hand-held electric beater, for 5–10 minutes until pale and thick and the beater leaves a trail in the mixture. Remove from the heat and fold in the melted butter and half of the lemon rind.
3. Sift the flours together, then fold into the beaten mixture. Divide between the prepared pans and bake in a 375°F oven for about 15 minutes, until risen and firm to the touch.
4. Meanwhile, make the syrup. Place the lemon juice, remaining sugar and the water in a saucepan. Heat gently until the sugar has dissolved, then bring to the boil and boil until it reaches 220°F on a candy thermometer, or until thickened and syrupy.
5. Spoon over the sponge cakes and leave in the pans until cold.
6. Beat the lemon curd with the remaining lemon rind, then fold in the cream. Sandwich the cakes together with about a third of the cream.
7. Reserve about 6 tablespoons of the remaining cream. Cover the top and side of the cake with the rest. If you wish, run a serrated icing comb around the side to give a decorative finish.
8. Sprinkle the pistachios all over the cake.
9. Fill a piping bag fitted with a star tip with the reserved cream and pipe rosettes around the top edge of the cake. Cut the sliced lemon into tiny triangles and place one on each rosette.

VARIATION

Orange. Substitute the grated rind and juice of 2 small oranges for the lemons. Use orange curd for the flavored cream and decorate with orange slices instead of lemon slices.

JANIE'S FAVORITE CHOCOLATE CAKE

1¾ cups all-purpose flour
1 tablespoon baking powder
¼ teaspoon salt
1 teaspoon ground cinnamon
¼ teaspoon ground cloves
1 cup chopped walnuts
4 oz baker's semi-sweet chocolate
6 tablespoons water
½ cup butter
1 cup superfine sugar
4 eggs, separated

FOR THE FILLING AND TOPPING:
1 quantity Creme au Beurre, flavored with 3 tablespoons chocolate or orange liqueur*
3 oz baker's semi-sweet chocolate

Serves 12–16
Preparation time: About 1 hour
Cooking time: About 30 minutes
Freezing: Recommended, at end of stage 5

1. Grease two 10 inch round cake pans and line the bases.
2. Sift all the dry ingredients together, then stir in the walnuts.
3. Place the chocolate and water in a small saucepan and heat gently until melted. Leave to cool.
4. Cream the butter with half of the sugar until pale and fluffy. Beat in the remaining sugar, then the egg yolks. Beat in the chocolate until well mixed.
5. Beat the egg whites until stiff, then fold into the mixture, alternately with the dry ingredients. Transfer to the prepared pans and bake in a 350°F oven for about 30 minutes, until risen and firm to the touch. Cool on a rack.
6. Sandwich the cakes together with about a quarter of the creme au beurre. Use the rest to cover the top and side of the cake.
7. Peel layers from the chocolate with a potato peeler to make short curls. Sprinkle over the cake to decorate.

WALNUT AND RASPBERRY GATEAU

It is best to leave this gateau in a cool place for a few hours after assembling, but decorate the top just before serving.

4 eggs
½ cup superfine sugar
1 cup all-purpose flour
1 teaspoon baking powder
1¼ cups finely chopped walnuts, toasted
2 tablespoons butter, melted
1¾ cups raspberries
2½ cups heavy cream, lightly whipped
12 pieces angelica

1. Grease three 8 inch round cake pans and line the bases.
2. Place the eggs and sugar in a large bowl over a pan of simmering water and beat with an electric beater for 5–10 minutes, until pale and the beater leaves a trail across the surface of the mixture. Remove from the heat.
3. Sift the flour and baking powder together, then stir in the walnuts. Carefully fold into the beaten mixture. Fold in the butter.
4. Divide the mixture between the prepared pans and bake in a 350°F oven for 20–25 minutes, until risen and firm to the touch. Cool on a rack.
5. Reserve 12 raspberries for decoration. Fold the rest into half of the cream; use to sandwich the cakes together.
6. Transfer the cake to a serving plate and cover the top and side with three-quarters of the remaining cream.
7. Put the remaining cream in a piping bag fitted with a star tip and pipe scrolls on top of the cake.
8. Decorate with the reserved raspberries and angelica.

Serves 10–12
Preparation time: 45 minutes
Cooking time: 20–25 minutes
Freezing: Recommended, at end of stage 7

MAPLE SYRUP ICE CREAM ROLL

Maple syrup has a delicate and delicious flavor which goes very well with butter pecan ice cream.

3 eggs
6 tablespoons maple syrup
2/3 cup all-purpose flour
1 tablespoon cornstarch
18 fl oz carton butter pecan ice cream
superfine sugar for sprinkling

Serves 8
Preparation time: 25 minutes
Cooking time: 7–8 minutes
Freezing: Essential!

1. Grease and line a 13 × 9 inch jelly roll pan with waxed paper.
2. Place the eggs and maple syrup in a large bowl over a pan of simmering water. Using a hand-held electric beater, beat until really thick and pale and the beater leaves a trail in the mixture.
3. Sift the flours together, then fold into the mixture.
4. Transfer to the prepared pan and bake in a 400°F oven for 7–8 minutes, until risen and firm to the touch.
5. Dampen a clean dish cloth, place it on the work surface and cover with a piece of waxed paper about the same size as the jelly roll pan. Sprinkle with superfine sugar.
6. Invert the sponge cake onto the sugared paper, leaving the pan in position. Leave until cold, then remove the pan and lining paper.
7. Soften the ice cream slightly and work to a spreadable consistency. Spread the ice cream to within ½ inch of the edges of the sponge and roll up, starting from a short edge. Freeze immediately until required.
8. Trim the ends and sprinkle with superfine sugar to serve.

ALMOND FILBERT DACQUOISE

The easiest way to brown the nuts for this recipe is to roast them on separate baking sheets in a 350°F oven for 15–20 minutes until golden.

3/4 cup blanched whole almonds, browned and ground
1 cup filberts, browned and ground
5 egg whites
1 cup superfine sugar
2 teaspoons cornstarch
1 1/4 cups heavy cream, lightly whipped
3/4 cup browned slivered almonds
1 tablespoon sifted powdered sugar
strawberries to decorate

1. Draw a heart-shape template about 9 inches across and 7 inches at its highest point on a piece of cardboard. Cut it out and draw round it on 3 pieces of waxed paper. Place on 3 baking sheets.
2. Mix the ground almonds with half of the filberts.
3. Beat the egg whites until stiff, then beat in the sugar a tablespoon at a time. Fold in the cornstarch and mixed nuts.
4. Divide the mixture between the heart-shapes and spread evenly to within the drawn lines. Bake in a 300°F oven for 1¾–2 hours, until crisp and dry. Leave to cool.
5. Fold the remaining filberts into half of the cream and use to sandwich the hearts together.
6. Place the heart on a flat board and cover the top and sides with the remaining cream. Press the slivered almonds over the top and sides and dust with the powdered sugar.
7. Carefully transfer the cake to a serving platter and decorate the center with strawberries.

Serves 10–12
Preparation time:
50 minutes
Cooking time:
1¾–2 hours
Freezing:
Not recommended

BUTTERSCOTCH PECAN TORTE

½ cup light brown sugar, packed
3 eggs, separated, plus 1 yolk
1 cup ground pecan nuts, toasted
1 tablespoon dried white breadcrumbs
pinch of salt
10 pecan halves to decorate

FOR THE BUTTERSCOTCH CREAM:
1 tablespoon golden syrup or ½ tablespoon each light corn syrup and molasses
2 tablespoons butter
¼ cup light brown sugar, packed
1¼ cups heavy cream

Serves 10
Preparation time: 45 minutes
Cooking time: About 25–30 minutes
Freezing: Recommended

1. Grease an 8½ inch springform pan and line the base.
2. Beat three-quarters of the sugar and the egg yolks together until pale. Fold in the nuts and breadcrumbs.
3. Beat the egg whites with the salt until stiff, then beat in the remaining sugar. Fold into the nut mixture.
4. Transfer the mixture to the prepared pan and bake in a 350°F oven for about 25–30 minutes, until risen and firm to the touch. Cool on a rack.
5. To make the butterscotch cream, place the syrup, butter and sugar in a pan and heat gently until melted. Add 3 tablespoons of the cream and bring to the boil. Place the pan in a bowl of cold water to cool, stirring constantly.
6. Beat the remaining cream until stiff, then carefully fold in the butterscotch sauce; *do not beat.*
7. Split the cake in half horizontally and sandwich together with a quarter of the butterscotch cream.
8. Use all but about 5 tablespoons of the remaining cream to cover the top and side of the cake in a swirled pattern.
9. Place the remaining cream in a piping bag fitted with a star tip and pipe 10 swirls on top of the cake. Press a pecan half onto each.

VARIATION

Maple Walnut Torte. Replace the pecans with walnuts. For the cream, replace the golden syrup, butter and sugar with ¼ cup maple syrup. Fold into the whipped cream and decorate with walnut halves.

BRANDIED COFFEE GATEAU

This cake is soaked in brandy-flavored coffee while still warm, then allowed to cool in the pan. Topped with whipped cream it makes a delicious dessert. Any spirit or liqueur may be used instead of brandy.

1/2 cup butter
1/2 cup light brown sugar, packed
2 eggs, beaten
1 cup sifted self-rising flour
1/2 cup chopped walnuts
1 1/4 cups strong fresh coffee
1 teaspoon gelatin
1/4 cup brandy
1 cup heavy cream, whipped
walnut halves to decorate

Serves 10
Preparation time:
35 minutes
Cooking time:
25–30 minutes
Freezing:
Recommended, at end of stage 5

1. Grease a 7 inch loose-bottomed round cake pan and line the base.
2. Cream the butter and sugar together until pale and fluffy. Beat in the eggs a little at a time, then fold in the flour and walnuts.
3. Transfer the mixture to the prepared pan and bake in a 350°F oven for 25–30 minutes, until risen and firm to the touch.
4. Place about 3 tablespoons of the coffee in a small pan. Sprinkle over the gelatin, leave to soak for a few minutes, then heat gently until dissolved. Add the remaining coffee and brandy and stir well.
5. Pour the coffee mixture over the cake while it is still hot. Leave in the pan until cold.
6. Transfer to a serving plate and cover with the whipped cream, swirling it attractively. Decorate with walnut halves to serve.

CHESTNUT MOUSSE GATEAU

4 eggs, separated
1/2 cup superfine sugar
16 oz can unsweetened chestnut puree
1 tablespoon hot water
1/2 cup ground almonds
1/4 cup fresh breadcrumbs
2 teaspoons baking powder
1 1/4 cups heavy cream
1 tablespoon powdered sugar
1 tablespoon brandy
1/2 teaspoon cocoa powder
10 small pieces marron glacé or 10 small chocolates to decorate

1. Grease an $8\frac{1}{2}$ inch springform cake pan and line the base.
2. Using an electric beater, beat the egg yolks and sugar together until thick and pale. Beat in the chestnut puree and hot water.
3. Mix the ground almonds, breadcrumbs and baking powder together, then fold into the beaten mixture.
4. Beat the egg whites until stiff, then fold into the mixture. Transfer to the prepared pan and bake in a 350°F oven for 50 minutes to 1 hour, until just firm to the touch. Cool on a rack.
5. Whip the cream and powdered sugar together until it just holds its shape. Fold in the brandy.
6. Split the cake in half horizontally; sandwich together with a quarter of the cream. Place on a serving plate.
7. Use just more than two-thirds of the remaining cream to cover the top and side of the cake. Sprinkle the surface with the cocoa powder.
8. Use the remaining cream to pipe 10 rosettes around the edge of the cake and top each with a piece of marron glacé or a chocolate.

Serves 10
Preparation time: 20 minutes
Cooking time: 50–60 minutes
Freezing: Recommended, at end of stage 4

BASIC TECHNIQUES

BASIC INGREDIENTS

Flour. Both white and whole wheat flours may be used successfully in cake making. Whole wheat flour will give a nuttier flavor, especially good in gingerbreads, but perfectly acceptable in a sponge cake.

If using white flour always sift it, with any baking powder, salt and spices, to aerate and remove any lumps. I have used mainly all-purpose flour and baking powder or baking soda in preference to self-rising flour to give the exact aeration and rise required for each cake.

A proportion of cornstarch, arrowroot or potato flour may be used in an all-purpose flour recipe if a softer texture is preferred.

Shortening. I have specified butter in most recipes as it has such a good flavor, but you may use margarine if you prefer. Oil may also be used and is particularly good if you want to cook a cake in a microwave oven as it helps to keep a moist soft texture.

Sugar. Use a fine-grained sugar such as superfine or brown. Granulated or light brown granulated sugar will give a coarser, slightly granular texture, which may be preferred with some small cakes.

Honey or molasses, maple or light corn syrup may also be used for sweetening, preferably with a proportion of sugar to give a good texture.

Eggs and liquid. These should be kept at room temperature before use.

BASIC METHODS

Rubbing in. Shortening is rubbed into flour until the mixture resembles fine crumbs. The remaining dry ingredients are added, then the egg and liquid are stirred in. Don't beat, or the mixture will toughen and result in a heavy cake. This method is used for plainer cakes.

Melting. The shortening and liquid are melted together, cooled, then added to the dry ingredients. Make sure that the mixture is cooled before adding or the flour will start to cook and the cake will be tough. This method is used for gingerbread.

Creaming. Softened shortening is beaten with sugar until very pale and fluffy—the mixture should fall easily from the beaters when tapped against the side of the bowl. It is this initial creaming which gives the cake its light moist texture—lack of creaming produces a dry firm cake. If more sugar than shortening is used, cream the shortening with an equal amount of sugar first then add the rest.

Beat in the eggs a little at a time, then fold in the flour. (Beating the mixture once the flour has been added makes it elastic and results in a tough-textured cake.) A Victoria sandwich is the classic cake made by this method.

Beating. Eggs and sugar are beaten together in a large bowl over a pan of simmering water, using an electric beater, until really thick and pale and the beater leaves a trail—this will take 5–10 minutes. Remove from the water and beat until cool. Fold in the flour, then the cooled melted butter. This results in a soft-topped, slightly sticky sponge cake.

CREME AU BEURRE

This is a creamy butter frosting which uses an egg custard as its base. Be sure to use sweet butter or the frosting will be very salty.

1/3 cup superfine sugar
3 egg yolks
1/3 cup milk
3/4 cup sweet butter, diced

1. Using an electric beater, beat the sugar and egg yolks together until thick and pale.
2. Bring the milk just to the boil, then beat into the egg mixture.
3. Transfer to a small pan and cook gently, stirring constantly, until the mixture thickens just enough to coat the back of the spoon.
4. Remove from the heat immediately, strain into a mixing bowl and continue beating until tepid.
5. Beat the butter into the egg custard a little at a time until thick.
6. Beat in any flavorings at this stage. Use as required to fill and decorate cakes.

Makes sufficient to fill and top an 8–9 inch cake
Preparation time: 25 minutes
Freezing: Not recommended, unless used to complete a cake

VARIATIONS

Liqueur. Flavor with 2–3 tablespoons of your favorite liqueur.

Coffee or vanilla. Beat in 1–2 tablespoons strong coffee or 1–2 teaspoons vanilla to taste.

Chocolate. Beat in 2 oz melted cooled baker's semi-sweet chocolate.

Citrus. Beat in finely grated citrus rind and juice to taste.

Fruit. Beat in a little thick fruit puree, e.g. strawberry, raspberry, dried apricot, date or prune.

JAM GLAZE

Jam glaze is used to brush over fresh fruits to give them an attractive finish, or to attach almond paste to a cake. Store in a screw-topped jar or rigid plastic container in the refrigerator for up to 2 months.

1 cup strawberry or apricot jam
2 tablespoons water
squeeze of lemon juice

Makes about 1 cup
Preparation time: 10 minutes
Freezing: Not recommended

Place the ingredients in a saucepan and heat gently, stirring, until the jam has melted, then boil for 1 minute. Strain, cool and use as required.

VARIATION

Redcurrant. Use redcurrant jelly, without water. No need to strain.

ALMOND PASTE

Home-made almond paste is very different from store bought marzipan. It is moist, subtly flavored—and easy to make. It will keep for about 2 weeks in the refrigerator.

2 cups ground almonds
1 cup sifted powdered sugar
½ cup superfine sugar
1–2 egg whites
1 teaspoon lemon juice
½ teaspoon orange flower water or almond extract

Makes about 1 lb
Preparation time: 15 minutes
Freezing: Not recommended

1. Mix the ground almonds and sugars together in a large bowl.
2. Add 1 egg white, the lemon juice and orange flower water or almond extract and mix to a firm paste, adding extra egg white if necessary.
3. Wrap in plastic wrap and chill until required.

CREME PATISSIERE

2 tablespoons all-purpose flour
2 tablespoons cornstarch
¼ cup superfine sugar
1¼ cups milk
2 egg yolks
⅔ cup heavy cream, whipped

1. Sift the flours into a bowl, stir in the sugar, then add about 2 tablespoons of the milk. Stir well to make a thick paste. Beat in the egg yolks.
2. Heat remaining milk in a saucepan to just below boiling point. Pour onto the egg mixture, stirring constantly.
3. Strain back into the saucepan and cook gently, stirring constantly, until thickened. Leave until cold, beating occasionally to prevent a skin forming.
4. Fold in the cream. Use as required to fill cakes.

Makes about 2 cups
Preparation time: 20 minutes
Freezing: Not recommended

FRANGIPANE CREAM

2 tablespoons all-purpose flour
2 tablespoons cornstarch
2 tablespoons superfine sugar
$1\frac{1}{4}$ cups milk
2 egg yolks
$\frac{2}{3}$ cup heavy cream, whipped
$1\frac{1}{2}$ cups crushed macaroons

1. Sift the flours into a bowl, stir in the sugar, then add about 2 tablespoons of the milk. Stir well to make a thick paste. Beat in the egg yolks.
2. Heat the remaining milk in a saucepan until just below boiling point. Pour onto the egg mixture, stirring constantly.
3. Strain back into the saucepan and cook gently, stirring constantly, until thickened. Leave until cold, beating occasionally to prevent a skin forming.
4. Fold in the cream and crushed macaroons. Use as required.

Makes about 2 cups
Preparation time: 25 minutes
Freezing: Not recommended

CHOCOLATE GANACHE

This is a rich chocolate frosting made simply from chocolate and fresh cream. Add flavorings of your choice, such as rum or orange liqueur, to give a boost to the flavor.

1 cup heavy cream
8 oz baker's semi-sweet chocolate, broken into pieces

1. Place the cream and chocolate in a saucepan and heat gently, stirring, until the chocolate has melted.
2. Transfer to a mixing bowl and leave for at least 1 hour, to cool.
3. Beat until smooth and fluffy. Use as required, to fill and decorate cakes.

Preparation time: 15 minutes, plus cooling time
Freezing: Recommended

INDEX

Photography by: Andy Seymour
Designed by: Sue Storey
Home economist: Jane Suthering
Stylist: Penny Legg
Illustration by: Linda Smith
U.S. Consultant Editor: Carla Capalbo